If These Walls Could Talk

If These Walls Could Talk

TANYA COOK

StoryTerrace

Disclaimer This book includes stories that feature gay and bi-sexual individuals acting in stereotypically 'macho' male roles, which the authors would like to acknowledge is not a fair portrayal. This decision was made deliberately to help male readers achieve greater understanding of the uncomfortable feeling women experience when they find themselves in similar situations. It is our hope that by inspiring these emotional reactions, men will become more aware of how their words and actions can lead to a hostile work environment that affects others' ability to perform at their highest levels.

Text Wendy Strain, on behalf of StoryTerrace
Design StoryTerrace
Copyright © Tanya Cook and StoryTerrace
Text is private and confidential

First print August 2021

StoryTerrace
www.StoryTerrace.com

CONTENTS

1. DAVID AND THE DANGERS OF
   A HOSTILE WORK ENVIRONMENT   7

2. KEVIN AND THE CONSEQUENCES
   OF INAPPROPRIATE TOUCHING   23

3. MARK AND THE PERILS OF
   COMPROMISE   41

1

DAVID AND THE DANGERS OF A HOSTILE WORK ENVIRONMENT

"Next round's on me!" Eric called out to the waitress, circling his hand above the table of six young men. A collective cheer rose up as glasses at various levels of almost empty were raised.

David drank in the moment. It felt good to have his buddies celebrate his good fortune.

Two years of hustle earned him enough of a reputation to have one of the biggest software firms in the city seek him out. They pulled out all the stops to entice him, offering 40% greater pay and a package of benefits his former company never dreamed of. Plus, his new company was international. With plenty of room for growth and his own talent, David knew he'd move up the ranks quickly. He expected he'd achieve management level within a year or two. His star was on the rise.

The new round of beer was delivered by a petite blonde waitress who angled herself to face David as she transferred the glasses from her tray to the table, giving him a wink in the process. Surprised, he gave her a smile back before she left, peeking adorably over her shoulder as she went.

He felt a nudge from his buddy on the other side.

"I think she's into you, man," Greg said.

"Yeah, you should get her number," Eric pitched in.

"I'd totally hit that," John slurred.

The rest of the guys started swatting at John, half in play.

"Not cool," Greg scolded. "Have some respect."

Meanwhile, David glanced back at the register, where their waitress was greeting some new customers. Maybe he would ask for her number. She looked like someone he'd like to know better.

Just as he was formulating his plan for casually making this bar his new hangout spot, their waitress brushed by him on her way back to the kitchen, stuffing a scrap of paper into his hand as she went. Opening it up, he saw a name and a number. Smiling, he tucked it into his pocket and enjoyed the ribbing from his friends.

Monday morning, he reported to his new building full of expectation. Riding the elevator up, he was already drafting ideas for how he'd prove to the company his reputation was well-deserved. But when he stepped off the elevator, the open office plan he encountered was disorienting enough to throw him off. His last job had been cubicles arranged in an obvious way, pointing out the path to the floor manager's office.

"You must be the new guy," a man passing nearby commented, looking David up and down with a critical eye. "You'll want to talk to Pete, over there," and he pointed in the general direction of a group of men talking off to the right.

Still slightly confused, David gave a nod of thanks and headed that direction. Looking back to make sure he was heading for the right group, it seemed the other man was checking out his backside while he walked away. Within a blink, the man smiled and waved him on. David decided he must be imagining things.

The group of men all turned as he got near, and the one closest to him held out his hand.

"David, right? I'm Pete."

For the rest of the morning, Pete showed David around the office, which basically amounted to visiting a number of desks spaced throughout the open area, trying to remember several names at once, and where to find Pete's office, the restroom, and the break room. Throughout the entire tour, Pete alternated between spitting out office rules and procedures and giving David a rundown of each person they approached or walked away from as to their responsibilities and relation to David's position. They got to David's desk, which was stationed close to the break room, when Pete noticed it was lunchtime.

In celebration of David's first day, Pete had reserved a table at a nearby restaurant for the whole floor, about twenty people. At that point, David would have been happy with a burrito in his car just to have a few quiet moments to process everything, but he had to admit it was a good way to get to know some of his co-workers a little.

The man he'd met at the elevator turned out to be Steve, who also happened to be seated across the table from David at lunch. He introduced David to Michael and Frank, who sat to either side of him. Pete sat to one side of David, and Mary, another software engineer, sat to the other side. Conversation around the table was polite and casually professional, though neither David nor Mary had much to say.

Coming back into the office area, everyone seemed to head back to their desks to focus on their work without a lot of chatter. Pete went back to his office, and David figured this was getting back to business as usual. David settled into his desk space and started into his onboarding forms. Moving step-by-step through the monotonous forms, he easily lost track of time. He wouldn't have known it was break time if he hadn't heard voices talking nearby.

Glancing up, he could just see a man's arm bobbing around inside the open break room door as the men talked.

"Did you see that fine ass?" David thought that sounded like Steve's voice coming from inside the room.

"Hush, he might hear you." Was that Michael? Did he say *he*?

"I love it when we get fresh eye candy in here," a third

voice chimed in. "But I'm not sure he plays on our team."

They couldn't be talking about him, could they? David wondered.

"I don't care what team he plays on," that was definitely Steve. "I can look all I want."

Just then, David saw Frank peek out the doorway toward Pete's closed office door. As he moved to pop back into the break room, his eyes fell to meet David's, and he gave a start.

"I forgot his desk is right outside," David heard Frank hiss at the others. "I think he might be able to hear us."

"I've sat at that desk before," Michael said. "You can hear people talking, but you can't really tell what they're saying."

"Are you sure?" Frank asked. "He looked a little freaked out."

"Maybe he'll overhear us and decide to experiment," Steve giggled.

Now David was sure they were talking about him. He had never thought about being attractive to men before and wasn't at all comfortable with the idea, but at the same time, he was kind of proud to be considered good-looking.

"You're always trying to convert men," Michael chastised. "You know it doesn't work like that."

"What? You swing both ways. Maybe he just hasn't given it enough thought," Steve responded.

David didn't need any thought. He knew his own tastes, and they did not include men. He was feeling more uncomfortable that the guys were talking about him this way. Should he say something to them?

He glanced over toward Pete's office just in time to see the door swing open. At about the same moment, the voices in the break room stopped, and Steve, Michael, and Frank skirted out of the break room in David's peripheral vision. Looking back at them, David saw Steve give him a wink.

He was sure Steve had been checking him out back at the elevator that morning and was trying to flirt with him now. He felt a moment of panic as he wondered how aggressive Steve would get in what Michael phrased 'trying to convert men.'

Nothing else happened for the rest of the day, but David didn't manage to finish his onboarding forms by closing time either. He'd been too busy puzzling over what to do about Steve and examining Michael and Frank's behaviors at their desks. They seemed completely normal, but now David knew they slept with men. It was strange to him how that somehow altered the way he was thinking of them. He worried they were watching him when he wasn't looking.

By the end of the day, he decided it really didn't matter all that much. As Steve had said, David couldn't control where someone else's eyes went. It didn't actually hurt him any for Steve to look at him. He just hoped he would stop being the topic of conversation soon. He also decided it might be helpful to find ways to reinforce to the guys that he was most definitely a heterosexual man. What they talked about or what they looked at was really of no concern to him and shouldn't affect his job performance at all.

Chastising himself for not making the progress he should have made through the afternoon, David promised himself to be more focused the next day.

As the days moved on, things didn't get better. David remained the primary point of conversation among Steve's group in the break room for the better part of a month, except on Mondays, when Steve was usually telling the other two guys about his weekend exploits. It seemed like they were always in there talking about how David looked in his clothes, or wondering what he was working with below the belt, or they were sitting at their desks staring at David. If he had to hear Steve tell him how good he smelled one more time, he might just lose it. It didn't feel like the compliment he assumed Steve thought it was.

Even though he tried to ignore it, David realized he'd become very self-conscious about the way he moved around the office space. He tried as hard as he could to keep his butt in his chair, suddenly realized when his button-down shirt would gap open to reveal his chest if he had to bend over to throw something away, and learned he had a 'lionesque stride' when he arrived in the building each morning.

Rather than focusing on his work, David spent a lot of time at his desk trying to figure out whether he should say something to someone and, if so, who should it be and what would he say?

He was embarrassed to talk about the issue with his friends outside of work. They weren't on the same track he was and wouldn't understand the office politics. Trying to say something to Steve didn't seem like it would be very effective based on his responses to Michael and Frank when they sometimes tried to rein him in. There was a company policy about sexual harassment in the workplace, but David wasn't sure whether this qualified.

Besides, he was still the new guy. He didn't want to be the only one to file a formal complaint. What if it put a black mark on his record? Would he still be able to reach management levels if he started to complain now?

Hoping he might have some support, David started paying attention to what other people in the office were doing. No one else seemed to venture into the break room much other than to get something out of the refrigerator or purchase something from the snack machine. Most people seemed to take their breaks at their desks or leave the building for lunch. He tried to get to know a few of them more personally, but they rebuffed him, keeping their responses short and their heads down.

"Does it ever bother you that Steve, Michael, and Frank are always in the break room?" David asked Mary one day.

"Better there than out here," she said. And then she walked away.

That was as close as David got to hearing anyone else complain about the conversations the three men were having. Clearly, the other employees weren't happy with the guys' behavior any more than David was, but everyone else seemed capable of keeping their focus on their work.

He tried not to listen, but David learned more about the flamboyantly gay lifestyle than he ever wanted to know while he tried to concentrate on his work. It was almost impossible to ignore them, and he found days would go by when he got nothing done.

Maybe he could drown them out, he thought. He brought ear buds with him to work one day and happily settled into his desk to work. That was the one morning he felt truly productive, but Pete saw him before lunch and informed him ear buds were a violation of company policy.

Resigned to his fate, David decided the only thing he could do at this point was force his way through, but he hated coming to work in the morning. The guys even commented about how he'd lost his 'prideful stride' and had instead adopted an 'old man's shuffle.' David didn't care. He needed to try to focus on his work like the other employees on the floor did and just make it to the next level.

At the end of his first month, Pete called him into his office.

"David, I'm concerned about your work performance so far. Is everything OK?"

"What do you mean?" David knew exactly what Pete meant, but he'd been hoping no one had noticed.

"You were hired because you were supposed to be a

crackerjack software engineer," Pete said, "but so far, I've seen very little progress on your programs. You come in a little later every day and leave a little earlier. I even caught you one day with ear buds, trying to check out of work while on the clock. What's going on with you?"

David knew this was his opportunity to say something about the guys in the break room and how disruptive their language and their unwanted attention to his every move was to his concentration. But if no one else had complained about the guys, would Pete think he was just making excuses for his poor performance?

"W-w-would it be possible to move to a different desk?" he asked instead.

At the look of surprise on Pete's face, David hastened to provide an explanation that wouldn't get anyone in trouble.

"It's just that the break room is so close, and it's sometimes hard for me to stay focused on my work when people are coming and going," he explained, feeling like he already sounded a bit too needy.

"We don't have any other available desks at this time," Pete said, somewhat coldly. "Are you telling me you can't work here?"

"No!" He knew it was a mistake to say anything. "No, it isn't that. I-I'm just not used to the open office concept. It's taking me a little bit to adjust, but I can make it work," David said. As the words spilled out of his mouth, his visions of management and a cushy salary by 30 started to dissolve in his mind. He needed to keep this job if he was going to make that happen.

"I expect to see much more out of you in the near future, David," Pete said. "Your probation review is in just two months, and so far, I can't say I'm overly impressed."

Swallowing a giant lump in his throat, David made his way back to his desk, hearing the guys in the break room discussing a random hookup Steve had made the night before, including all the lurid details.

How could he possibly deal with all this and still keep Pete happy?

"Did you see him walking into Pete's office earlier?" Michael's voice drifted over David.

"I hope Pete's not getting rid of him already," Frank said. "We've barely had a chance to get to know him."

"He can't leave until I've gotten a taste of that. It's only a matter of time," Steve said.

David couldn't take it anymore. Something had to be done or he'd lose his job, and he didn't want to panic about what might happen if he found himself alone with Steve. He got up and boldly walked into the break room.

"Well, look what the cat dragged in," Steve said with an appreciative smile on his face.

Michael and Frank had the decency to look embarrassed.

Actually facing the guys, David suddenly didn't know what to say. He couldn't just blurt out a request that they not talk about him anymore. Searching for something to say, he instead went to the coffee machine and began preparing a cup, keenly aware of the eyes boring into his back and the pregnant silence behind him.

Holding his coffee cup like a shield, he turned around to face them again, plastering a friendly grin across his face.

"So, you guys have a good weekend?" he asked casually.

"Yeah, yeah, mowing the grass, nice weather," Frank offered, somewhat trailing for what to say.

"Sure, went out with a few friends," Michael offered.

"I had a hot date," Steve said boldly.

David already knew all about that date. Before Steve could offer details, David seized on the opportunity.

"Yeah? Me too! I met this beautiful blonde waitress at a bar not too long ago, and we were finally able to meet up. It's hard because she usually works on the weekends, but she traded with a friend."

He tried hard not to put too much emphasis on the 'she' references, but he certainly wanted to emphasize his taste was in women.

"Where'd you take her?" Frank asked politely.

"I hope you gave her a nice evening," Michael said. David wondered if there was a hint of suggestion in his tone but decided to ignore it.

"But was it hot?" Steve asked.

"I don't know what you mean," David said, though he had a good idea.

"Did you bang her?" Steve prodded. "It isn't a hot date unless you bang them."

"Uh, well, um, we're still just getting to know each other."

"Oh, honey," Steve said, "You've got to grab those opportunities when they're in front of you." He brushed close to David's body, winking and taking in a deep breath, as Frank led them out the door.

David was too shocked to respond to Pete's comment as he came in for a snack, but he did interpret the cocked eyebrow as a signal to get back to work.

By lunch, David had decided he needed to be a little more emphatic in his heterosexual status. Again, he waited until the guys were happily engaged in their normal lunchtime chatter before he went in with his brown bag lunch.

"Hi guys," he said, casually taking a seat at the table. "You don't mind if I join you, do you? I'm still trying to get settled in here."

A chorus of nos and welcomes echoed around the table as Steve hooked a foot around David's ankle. David shifted his feet away.

"So tell us more about your date," Frank prodded.

"Well, I took her to dinner at Luigi's Restaurant downtown," David started.

"No, we want to hear the juicy bits," Michael interrupted.

"After the movie, she invited me up for a drink," David offered.

"That's it. Then what?"

This was his chance to prove to them that he was 100% into girls. David launched into a blow-by-blow description of what he fantasized might have happened. The guys were paying rapt attention, and David got carried away.

"Her tits were so big," he said, holding his hands out in front of him. "And soft. I just buried my face in them and squeezed until she squealed. She tried to push me off, but I moved on down to her panties..." "Ahem," Pete's voice sounded from behind him.

All four men at the table gave a jump to look up at the supervisor standing authoritatively in the doorway with an angry woman standing next to him.

"David, you will come with me," Pete said.

Face flaming, David followed Pete to his office for the second time that day.

Once the door was shut, Pete turned to face David, neither of them taking a seat.

"I'm sure you are aware that kind of talk is not appropriate in an office setting," Pete said.

"Yes sir," David mumbled.

"It is against our company policy for anyone to demonstrate disrespect for other people's person. We have a zero-tolerance policy on such matters."

David looked up from the spot on the floor he'd been staring at. Did that mean what he thought it meant?

"I'm sorry, David, but between your poor work performance and what I just heard in the break room, I cannot allow you to remain in our employ. Do you have anything you wish to say for yourself before I write up the grounds for your dismissal?"

David practically fell into one of the chairs in front of Pete's desk. All his dreams were gone. He'd never get such a lucrative job again, especially not with this on his record.

But he couldn't deny what Pete had heard. Those words really had come out of his own mouth. There was no defense.

"No, sir, you are right. I knew better and there is no excuse for it," David mumbled, trying to get his thoughts in line. "I honestly don't know what came over me. I never talk like that, even to my closest friends. I love and respect women. I guess I just felt I needed to prove something to those guys."

Pete barked out a rough laugh. "You're talking to the wrong crowd there, kid."

David looked up, realizing Pete knew about their individual preferences as well. But how much did he know?

"I'm not asking for any leniency or trying to excuse my behavior," he offered hesitantly, "but do you know what it's like to sit at that desk and have to listen to them talking all day?"

"They don't use that kind of locker room talk at the office," Pete said. "You are welcome to have any orientation you wish, but you should know better than to bring that kind of language into the workplace."

"But they do," David argued. "All day, every day for the

past month I've had to listen to them discuss me, other men; they do it all the time."

"Why didn't you say something to me?" Pete asked. "As I said, we have a zero-tolerance policy on this kind of thing."

"I guess I was just too afraid of being the only one to complain."

"And now you're the only one out of work." Pete looked genuinely sorry. "I wish there was something I could do, but that woman you saw me with earlier is my boss. She will never let this slide."

By afternoon break, David did not have to hear himself as the topic of conversation in the break room. He was already on the street outside with a box full of his personal belongings.

2

KEVIN AND THE CONSEQUENCES OF INAPPROPRIATE TOUCHING

Kevin's hopes faded as he watched friends and family members depart by the hour as the NFL draft wore on. It was already day three, and the final-round choices were being made. Only five teams left.

He knew it was stupid to wish some of his friends would check in with him even though they weren't at the house anymore. Everyone had been instructed, under pain of pummeling (only half joking), not to call his phone until the draft was over. It didn't make him feel better to overhear the disheartened tone of voice as those still gathered fielded the inquiries coming in.

Unfortunately, the only time Kevin's phone rang over the past three days were spam calls. Each time, his heart rate jumped into the stratosphere, all eyes turned his way, gleaming with anticipation. And each time, he had to push the spammer off his phone while watching those eyes deaden with disappointment before they turned away.

And each day, fewer people gathered at his parent's house waiting for The Call. At this point, the only people left in his mother's living room were his mother and father, sister and brother, Vanessa and a couple of his brother's friends, his sister's friend Tiffany, and his aunt and uncle who lived on the street.

"Don't worry, son," his dad said, patting him on the shoulder at the dining table. "The draft isn't over yet, and you might get picked up as a free agent."

"Thanks, Dad," Kevin said. "If only the collarbone hadn't happened."

His dad just nodded, patted his shoulder again, and walked away. There was nothing much to say about the injury Kevin sustained his sophomore year of college. Many football injuries could be treated quickly these days, getting players back on the field within a few months, but a broken collarbone still needed time to heal, especially for a linebacker. One broken bone in the wrong spot and he was riding the bench his entire junior year.

Up to that point, he was the district favorite most likely to go pro. If it hadn't been for Vanessa helping him through physical therapy, he might not have returned to the game his senior year. She convinced him he still had a shot. He risked a covert glance in her direction. She was looking back at him, and they shared a secret smile.

One day, when they figured out how to get past their families' mutual racial mistrust, he could see himself marrying her. The problem was, her parents were South Korean and didn't trust Black folks, while his family resented the Asians for owning most of the businesses in their communities.

For now, she was just one of the girls that hung out with his older brother's crowd. It was killing him to have her so close and not be able to get close to her. He was considering going to sit on the arm of the couch next to her just to see how the family would react.

That's when the phone rang.

The entire family jumped at the sound. Glancing at the screen, the number wasn't recognized.

"H-hello," Kevin answered. He expected it to be another spam call, but with only a few more teams left to make their choices, he almost couldn't breathe through his tight nerves.

"Kevin Richardson?" an unfamiliar voice responded to his answer.

"Yes."

"This is Coach Jones from the Detroit Lions calling."

Kevin nearly dropped the phone but managed to hold on just enough to hear Coach Jones offer him a position on the team.

He listened to his instructions for a few moments. As soon as they realized it wasn't just another spam call, everyone in the house gathered around in anticipation, eyes riveted as he listened. As he started to smile, they started bouncing on the balls of their feet.

Hitting the End Call button on his screen, Kevin let loose

a loud whoop. When he cheered, his family joined in before the questions started at rapid-fire.

"Who was it?" his mom asked.

"The Detroit Lions?" his brother teased. "It could be worse."

Tyrone wrapped him in a big brother bear hug so he wouldn't have to deal with the rest of the questions, and Kevin high-fived everyone else, including Vanessa, in spite of a strong urge to sweep her up in his arms and swing her around.

Even with them both set to graduate with their degrees next month, neither of them were ready to tackle their families' issues just yet. Instead, he tried to convey his gratitude and love for her through his eyes in the split second they were able to connect before his family closed in again.

From the smile on her face, he guessed she knew.

Once all the excitement died down and the guests left for home, Kevin worked to help his sister clean up from the three days' worth of mess that accumulated since the draft began. He rinsed dishes and placed them in the dishwasher as Kiki worked to clear the table and bring dishes in from other rooms.

"I just don't understand what he sees in her," Kiki said as she wiped down the table.

"Who sees what in who?" Kevin asked.

"Ty," Kiki said. "I don't know why he keeps on bringing

that Asian girl over here. Can't he just date one of our own?"

Kevin felt a little awkward. This was the whole reason he kept his relationship with Vanessa quiet. Thank goodness Ty knew about their relationship and kept giving Vanessa excuses to come over. In spite of his continued denials, she had become so regular the family was now convinced Ty and Vanessa were a thing.

Confronted with his sister's question, Kevin had no idea how to respond.

"You should totally date my friend, Tiffany," Kiki said, switching topics mid-turn.

Kevin felt a little blindsided, although he shouldn't have. Kiki was never good at sticking to one topic, and she was always trying to get him to take Tiffany out. It was her pattern since their sophomore year of high school.

He liked Tiffany OK, but she wasn't anything compared to Vanessa. Tiffany had never been anything more than his sister's little friend, and he didn't think anything would change that.

"You know she's totally into you," Kiki said. "And you should get with a girl you know has substance before you head off to training camp. You'll have all those little gold diggers after you. You won't know who you can trust and who wants you for your money or your potential. You need someone who's been around for the worst of times, someone like Tiffany."

Kevin just kept rinsing the dishes. He knew his sister

well enough to know she'd just keep talking whether he responded or not. And there was nothing much he could say. His heart belonged to Vanessa. One day he would get up the courage to tell his family, but today was not that day.

Once the house was cleaned to his mother's satisfaction, Kevin gave his family one more hug goodbye before heading to his own apartment. His sister was right about one thing. The girls always threw themselves at the players, no matter how low on the draft they were. Getting invited to any of the team events off the field could get them sweet gifts, long-term lovers, and even introductions to their future husbands. How could he protect Vanessa from all of that while still keeping their secret?

These thoughts were still swirling in his head as he walked up to his door. That's when he saw the fancy Detroit Lions party bow stuck in the place a wreath should be. With a sly smile, he walked into his studio apartment to find his beautiful girlfriend sprawled seductively across his living room couch wearing nothing but blue and gray ribbons.

"Congratulations, baby," Vanessa purred, opening her arms to him.

Kevin dropped his keys on the nearby table and lost himself in his love for Vanessa.

Kevin arrived on his first day of rookie camp already tired of studying plays. He spent four days getting to know his coaches, trainers, and the other rookies on the team, walking through the plays and spending lots of time in the training room. He was anxious to make a great first impression and so far had done well. As a seventh-round draft pick, everyone knew the odds were against him, but his fellow rookies seemed to think he had a shot.

Vanessa flew up to Detroit for his weekend off with the excuse of having some physical therapy conference she wanted to attend, and they toured the Detroit Riverfront. He knew he shouldn't be taking a break from the plays, but he wanted her to know she would always come first in his book. Plus, he knew he wouldn't have a chance to see her for a month.

Real training camp started with the full team the following Monday. Training camp was full-on intensive, with the guys spending most of their time together on the field unless they were in the dorms studying. Looking at the itinerary, Kevin realized there would be a family day available, but as long as he was keeping Vanessa a secret from his family, he didn't think it would be a good idea to bring her out. There would be cameras and film crews there, and it would be hard to explain her appearance to the folks back home.

Instead, he dedicated himself 100% to the game. He ate a hearty breakfast, paid attention in the team meeting that followed, worked out hard during his strength training—the trainers were paying particular attention to his upper body strength after the collarbone incident—and played full-out during position drills. After lunch, he did his best to stop the offense in team drills and struggled to keep his attention focused through the afternoon meetings, studying the films and learning all he could about how his fellow teammates played the game.

Things with the team were pretty much as Kevin had experienced throughout his years as a football player. Of course, there was some hazing and some goofing around in the locker room, some practical jokes, and some guys he liked and some guys he could have done without. But he was determined to play the best game he could play, and that meant finding a way to get along with all the players on the team. The other guys gave him a hard time for being so good, which he considered to be a good thing. He was proving himself to be particularly good at understanding the playbook and making interceptions, which was becoming clear.

During one of the practice drills, for example, the offense ran a trick play in which the quarterback pitched to the running back, who faked a run for a few steps before passing the ball to a tight end cutting across the back field from the other side. Kevin saw this happening early and managed to cover the tight end, intercepting the pass with one hand.

Unfortunately, there was one player that gave Kevin an uncomfortable feeling. He couldn't quite put his finger on it, but his defensive end, John, seemed to pay Kevin more attention than the other members of the team. At first, Kevin thought John was just a nice guy trying to help the low man achieve his ambitions because he saw Kevin's potential to help the team win.

But the attention John gave Kevin seemed a little odd. Of course, Kevin was accustomed to regular locker room play among players. He'd been in the game since elementary school when he was first allowed to play and had been around sports for more than half of his life. Never once had it occurred to him to question the kind of physical attention one player gave to another. The occasional slap on the ass, a chest bump, even a sideways hug at random moments for a little too long was not unusual.

John was known to be more of a touchy-feely kind of guy, coming from California where everybody hugged, but he had helped to turn the team's prospects around over the past two years, so everyone just looked past it. Still, Kevin felt something was different. No matter what they were doing, John always seemed to find an excuse to touch him.

As the weeks went by, John's touching seemed to get even more physical. No matter what they were doing, he always found a reason to drape an arm across Kevin's shoulders or to slap his ass with a little too much force. Kevin was getting the distinct impression that John was somehow into him. As in, interested in a romantic relationship.

This was confusing because Kevin had seen John with his longtime girlfriend, Sarah. Sarah was one of the hottest girls anyone on the team had ever seen. Kevin had to be misinterpreting John's actions.

The truth came out one day on the field when Kevin drew another great play. Instead of a simple slap, John actually cupped his hand when touching Kevin's ass this time. That might have been fine if the action had come from Vanessa, but Kevin wasn't putting up with that from any man. He shoved John back harshly.

"Don't touch me anymore, man," he growled.

John threw his hands up in the air and backed off with a smile on his face.

"Just congratulating you, bro," he said. "Don't get your panties in a twist."

The other guys looked at Kevin strangely, as if his reaction had been inappropriate. From what they'd seen, Kevin guessed it probably appeared so to them. But after this, John started hanging out around Kevin's locker space in nothing but a towel, edging himself closer during practice, no matter how hard Kevin tried to avoid him.

Not sure how to deal with the situation or even how to pinpoint what the situation was, Kevin finally decided one day to confront John. He waited until the afternoon training meeting ended and everyone else was heading off to dinner before broaching the subject.

"John," Kevin began, "I appreciate your help including me on the team and getting up to speed with NFL expectations."

John smiled broadly and leaned almost seductively over the table for Kevin. "Yeah? You like my attention, do you?"

"About that, your attention gets pretty heavy sometimes. You need to back off." Kevin felt awkward. He had no idea how to put into words what was making him feel uncomfortable since he hadn't been able to define it for himself. John didn't seem to be doing anything more with him than with the other guys, and yet it felt like he was.

"Hello, you know me," John said with a flamboyant wave of his hand. "I'm just a hands-on kind of guy. None of the other guys seem to have a problem with it."

"Yeah, I guess," Kevin said, still struggling to find the words to express his feelings. "I just guess I come from a place where we aren't so hands-on. It makes me uncomfortable."

"Well, kid, I guess that's just something you're gonna have to get used to round here," John said with a smirk. He didn't give Kevin a chance to say anything else as he stood up and sauntered out of the room.

Kevin was at a loss. If he couldn't express his feelings to John clearly, how could he possibly talk to his coaches, trainers, or anyone else on the team about how uncomfortable he was with John's attention? All the other guys looked at John as if he were a god. How do you talk to hero worshipers about how their hero makes you feel when it's negative?

The next day at practice, the team was in a huddle, and somehow Kevin found himself standing next to John. It was a position he tried to avoid, so it surprised him. As the huddle broke up, Kevin felt a distinctive grab at his ass that went a little too deep between the legs. As he turned to figure out whether it had been an accident, he saw John walking at an angle toward another part of the field with a self-satisfied smirk on his face. When he saw Kevin looking at him, he smiled broader and gave Kevin a wink.

Kevin's play for the rest of that practice was sloppy and off time. The coaches yelled at him, the trainers yelled at him, his teammates yelled at him. Because of his performance, Kevin's coach kept him after practice to run extra drills. Exhausted, Kevin headed into the locker room as the rest of the guys were leaving.

"Suck it up, Buttercup," one of the players called out.

"Everyone has a rough day," another player called out. "Don't let it get you down."

"You better not bring that shit to the game," a third player yelled at him.

Feeling dejected, Kevin distractedly stripped off his sweaty practice gear, wrapped himself in a towel, grabbed his kit, and headed to the showers. Lathering up and rinsing off, he thought about his poor performance on the field and how he might go about preventing such distractions from throwing him off his game when it counted.

A soft noise behind him prompted Kevin to turn around. His eyes on the floor tiles swept the perimeter of the room until they found a pair of shoes standing near the entryway to the shower area. Moving up, he recognized John's figure before he even got to his face.

To Kevin's horror, John was staring intently at Kevin as

he showered. Who knew how long John had been standing there watching him? Leaning casually against the wall with his hands shoved deep in his pockets, John licked his lips as he continued to stare at Kevin, sweeping his eyes slowly down Kevin's torso until they landed at the sweet spot.

With a start, Kevin brought his hands to cover his genital area.

"What the hell?" Kevin uttered before he even had a chance to think about what he was going to say.

John just smiled wider as he licked his lips again.

"We'll see you again later," he said. With that, John disappeared into the dressing areas of the locker room.

Even more unsettled, Kevin wrapped a towel around himself without even finishing his shower. He looked around for another towel to cover more of himself but couldn't find one. Hastily, he made his way to his locker and got dressed in his street clothes without bothering to fully dry off.

By the last day of training camp, Kevin was feeling pretty good about his game play and his chances of staying on the team. His coaches and trainers seemed pleased with his progress, and he got along with most of the other players, though he was making a deliberate effort to stay as far away from John as he could. With John being his defensive end and leader of the defensive squad, that was a little more difficult than Kevin would have liked. Fortunately, there hadn't been many more incidents of John touching him since the shower, though Kevin still felt the man's eyes on him often. He took a certain amount of pleasure in knowing John was frustrated by Kevin's efforts to always keep another player between them and to rush his showers in the locker room only when other players were in the room.

The last day of training camp was the Blue and Gray scrimmage game with spectators scattered around Allen Park to see the team in action. It wasn't a real game, but it felt pretty close to it to Kevin. It was the last play of the game before they'd break for dinner, and Kevin was hyped up. This was his last chance to make an impression on his coaches and secure a spot on the team.

The offense opted to run a reverse, faking out the entire defensive team. John, as defensive end, had the contain, but even he missed the key signs. Kevin didn't. From his place on the field, he saw the fastest wide receiver on the team coming back across the field behind the line of scrimmage and instantly knew what was happening. While the rest of the defensive team went chasing after the running back, Kevin made a surprise open field tackle, popping the ball up and making another interception.

The team erupted! While some of the coaches and players were cheering for Kevin, others were screaming at the defensive team for not seeing the play happening, and others were yelling at the offense for not pulling off the play. Kevin wanted to bask in the glory of the moment but couldn't ignore the glare coming from John as a coach got up in his face. He was glad when some of the other players ushered him toward the locker room as a new team hero, leaving John mid-field with the coach still cussing at him, and the die-hard fans looking on.

Kevin was still feeling the glow as he sat down with the team for dinner, even though some of the guys were razzing him about maybe not making the team. He was, after all, still a seventh-round draft pick. It was easy to ignore it all until John joined in the ribbing. The others were clearly teasing, but John seemed dead serious. The comments he was throwing out were more personal, proving to Kevin, if not to anyone else, that John had been keeping an extra sharp eye on Kevin the whole time. He knew too many of Kevin's personal quirks, making comments disguised as generalized jibes. It didn't take long for Kevin's adrenaline-fueled buzz to morph into anger.

He had just enough self-control to remember that saying anything to John in front of the rest of the team would only hurt himself. While every muscle in his body was aching to beat the man into insensibility, or at least give it a good effort, Kevin exerted extreme control to march himself into the restroom to cool off for a second.

After splashing a little cold water on his face to stop seeing red, he moved over to the urinals, not even noticing when the door opened behind him. Before he knew what was happening, he'd been spun around and pressed back against the wall with John's body pressing hard against him and John's mouth planted firmly against Kevin's lips.

Kevin's shout of surprise was swallowed by John's tongue forcing its way inside.

"No!" Kevin shouted, pushing John against the opposite wall.

The red he'd only recently controlled came surging back with a vengeance as Kevin threw punch after punch at John's face and body, trying to beat the offensive touching off of himself. John fought back, getting a punch or two in around Kevin's fury, but something else was pulling at him.

Kevin continued to fight until he realized his other teammates had burst into the bathroom at the sound of the fight and pulled him off John. Other teammates were guarding John to make sure he wouldn't take a counter swing.

With dread, Kevin watched the head coach stalk in.

"What's going on in here?" he asked, looking at each man in turn.

"John came in, grabbed me, and stuck his tongue down my throat while I was taking a piss!" Kevin blurted out.

All eyes turned to John.

"C'mon, man," John drawled, wiping a trickle of blood from the corner of his mouth. "He just sucker punched me when I came in. Can't take a little teasing."

The rest of guys looked at each other uncomfortably, but no one said anything as they waited for the coach's response.

The coach looked sideways at John, apparently considering his response. Finally, he turned back to Kevin.

"Get your playbook. Meet me in my office."

Cut from the team on the spot, Kevin knew his chances at playing professional football were likely over.

After a few weeks at home to nurse his wounds, Vanessa finally convinced him to give the Canadian league a try. He'd still be playing and could keep in shape, and that would keep his options to return to the NFL next year or the year after as a free agent. It was a long shot, but that was all he had.

3

MARK AND THE PERILS OF COMPROMISE

Detrich didn't bother trying to suppress his groan when his roommate Carl walked into their shared dorm room with one of his gamer friends.

It didn't matter what night of the week it was. Carl always had a game night planned. Whether he brought a friend over or not, Detrich had to put up with nights full of whoops, hollers, grunts, and groans as his roommate worked his way through World of Warcraft, Fortnight, Final Fantasy, or whatever other game they decided to get mixed up in.

The distractions made it almost impossible for Detrich to study, or just enjoy an hour of peace with his own thoughts. He hadn't thought it would be too bad to live in the freshman dorms again this year, other than the humiliation of not being able to find roommates to share an apartment his sophomore year of college. But that was before Carl. Now Detrich was working on a new plan.

If he could successfully pledge a fraternity, he could get a room in one of the frat houses, and maybe then he could get some quiet time. He'd narrowed his choices to just two houses. While Carl and his friend played their stupid game, Detrich browsed their internet sites again.

Epsilon Gamma Row was ranked as a social fraternity, providing a family and support for gay students on campus. Detrich liked the idea of having that kind of strong, family-style support. He loved the crimson and gold colors, matching his own favorite color combo. Their tiger mascot would be cool to wear around campus. But his own family had been super-cool and accepting of him when he came out in high school, so he didn't feel he needed the extra support of an external family. Plus, he didn't want to just be known as a gay guy. He preferred blending in. Since his goal was to get a little quiet time, a social fraternity might not be the best choice.

Beta Epsilon Omega, on the other hand, was focused on supporting students studying business-related fields. As a marketing major and first-generation college student, Detrich knew he needed the connections and insights they could give him. Their colors were midnight blue and white, more understated than the other fraternity, but he wasn't so sure about the mascot. What the heck was a kraken supposed to be, anyway? To him, it just looked like a large octopus. Slimy sea creatures weren't his idea of awesome mascots.

Still undecided, Detrich worried about how it might look

for him to try rushing both houses next to the dreaded possibility neither one would want him, leaving him stuck in the dorms with Carl the entire year. In the end, he visited both.

The first rush party was with Epsilon Gamma Row. It was a full-out party with all the flamboyance only a group of gay guys could pull off. Detrich had a good time and met another rushee, Mark, who was also planning to attend the Beta Epsilon Omega party in two days. Detrich felt relieved to know he wasn't the only sophomore rushing more than one frat.

The second party was more formal, with the rushes being introduced to the other members of the fraternity over hors d'oeuvres and punch. This was the kind of environment he was looking for—a serious place where he could relax and get some serious studying in. There was a lot of polite conversation before they were given a tour of the house. Detrich almost drooled over the prospect of having a room of his own in the beautifully restored Victorian mansion.

He was delighted to receive a bid from Beta Epsilon Omega, proudly emblazoned with the giant octopus kraken, only a few days later. Arriving to accept his bid, he was also happy to see his new friend, Mark, there.

"Welcome to Beta Epsilon Omega house," one of the fraternity brothers told them, pacing back and forth along the line of four pledges.

This guy was possibly the hottest strawberry blonde

Detrich had ever seen. He might have missed a few things the guy said with the distraction of this beautiful, powerful figure stalking before him. He might not have caught himself drooling quite so quickly, but his gaze drifted past Mark as the guy crossed the line.

Mark's goofy grin and the way he was standing—hands splayed on his hips, fingers seeming to push his pelvis forward from the back—straightened Detrich's back as he reminded himself not to be so obvious.

"Before you can be considered a full member of this fraternity, you will be required to know our full bylaws, procedures, and policies. Brother," the guy said, motioning to another guy behind him.

"Yes, Brother," a brown-haired guy with glasses mumbled as he began handing out greenbooks to each of the pledges.

"And now I'd like to introduce Mr. Bob Cortez, our senior advisor," the first guy said, making way for a shorter, weightier man in his mid-30s wearing a business suit.

Mr. Cortez provided them with a brief history of the fraternity itself and the foundation of their chapter there on campus. Then he gave the floor back to the red-haired guy, who proceeded to tell them about some of the major accomplishments that had come out of the fraternity to date.

Every once in a while, he turned to Mr. Cortez for confirmation of something he was saying.

After about an hour of standing there listening to all this information, Detrich was struggling to keep his feet from shifting too much. Small noises coming from the other guys in the line made him realize he wasn't the only one getting a little antsy.

"I think that's a good start for today," Mr. Cortez said, interrupting the hot guy's newest story. "We want to welcome you again to Beta Epsilon Omega house and remind you that in order to become one of us, you must prove your ability to honor our codes and contribute to our strong tradition. While the boys will undoubtedly give you some testing," he turned and looked wryly back at the brothers waiting in the background, "their role is to guide you along the path to membership and be sure you've learned the information in your greenbooks. There is a strict university policy against hazing. You will report anything inappropriate directly to me. Is that understood?"

While he nodded dutifully with the other pledges in line, Detrich noticed the looks of warning coming at them from the guys standing behind the advisor. Clearly, they had a different set of rules in mind. Holding his sigh inside, Detrich reminded himself he hadn't expected anything less.

"Good," Mr. Cortez finished. "Well, I'll leave you boys to your brothers and look forward to welcoming you in as new members soon."

Mr. Cortez shot one more warning look at the guys behind him and headed out the door.

There was an awkward moment of silence as they all waited for Mr. Cortez to get away from the house. As they watched his car pull into the street out front, Fire jumped up in front of the group again.

"OK, pledges, listen up. From now on, you are little brothers. You will each be assigned a big brother. Until you are full members, you will only refer to your brothers by the names we give you. I'm Fire. This is Big Brother Earth," he pointed to the brown-haired guy with glasses. "Big Brother Wind is the blonde guy back there, and Big Brother Water is the drip on the stool."

As hot as he was, Detrich was already hoping he would not be assigned to Fire. The guy seemed a little too full of himself and reminded Detrich of an unpleasant relationship he'd had his junior year of high school.

"Now we will assign you your names," Fire announced, giving each of the pledges a critical look. "You," he pointed at the slightly overweight guy next to Detrich. "You are now Hippo, and I assign you to Brother Water."

The lanky guy unfolded himself from the stool he'd been sitting on the whole time, exposing himself to be at least twice as tall as he'd seemed, and motioned to Hippo to follow him out of the room.

"Earth, have you seen the overbite on this guy?" Fire tossed over his shoulder at the brown-haired brother. "Gator here can be yours."

"I'll give Ostrich to you, Brother Wind," Fire said, pointing at Detrich.

A flush of embarrassment lit up Detrich's face as he

realized this was a dig at his long legs, but it quickly faded as he heard Fire's next comments.

"I'll take the Kitten and see what can be done with him."

Detrich shot a look over at Mark. While Detrich himself would have been upset at receiving that nickname, Mark seemed thrilled with the idea of being paired up with the devastatingly handsome Fire.

With a shrug, Detrich followed Big Brother Wind into another room where he would be receiving his instructions for the next few days.

It turned out pledging a frat house was even more distracting than having a gamer roommate. At odd hours of the day and night, Brother Wind came whooshing into Detrich's room, threw a sack over his head, and hustled him down the dorm corridors to a waiting van. Detrich wasn't allowed to remove the sack, but he could tell by the noises the other pledges were being gathered as well.

Then they would drive around for hours grilling him and the others on the information in the greenbook. If any of them got an answer wrong, all of them had to run behind the van for a while, holding onto a rope to give them direction. Hippo seemed to suffer the most for these excursions.

After these grueling sessions, Detrich and the other pledge brothers had to perform random tasks of menial labor for their frat brothers. One time it was dressing in frilly aprons and maid's caps to clean the house. Another time they had to wash all their frat brothers' cars in their underwear. Detrich's preference was working on the landscaping because then, at least, he could pretend his life was normal in his regular clothes. It was particularly difficult to put up with the paddlings when one of the big brothers threw out a random question about an obscure founder that Gator never could remember.

While Detrich kind of saw the point in grilling them on the greenbook and running when they got answers wrong, he saw no point in the other activities, especially when he had studying to do. He was having a hard enough time getting his schoolwork done with Carl and his infernal gaming. However, every time he saw the rooms he might be assigned once he was accepted, he found the power to swallow his pride and put up with the treatments.

After just a few weeks of this treatment, Brother Wind decided it was time for Detrich to start "earning his keep." What that meant, Detrich learned, was they would be using Detrich's car, and Detrich would be driving as Brother Wind lounged in the passenger seat and chatted up the Uber customers they picked up on Wind's shift. Wind, of course, kept all the money, while Detrich had to pay for the gas. Detrich considered making a complaint, but then learned all the other pledges were being recruited for incidental tasks like this as well. He supposed it was to test their loyalty.

Not too long after he started driving Wind's Uber calls, Detrich was dropping his big brother off at the frat house when he saw Mark coming out with a big grin on his face. Detrich had never felt particularly happy about working for his big brother with quite the same level of joy Mark seemed to be displaying.

"I guess your job isn't as bad as driving Uber all night for free," Detrich mentioned to him.

Mark giggled a little. "No, I'm pretty satisfied with my position," he said with a little extra emphasis on the word satisfied.

"Wait," Detrich paused, recognizing the code words. "You're not... you aren't hooking up with him, are you?"

Mark giggled again. "Maybe just relieving a little stress, if you know what I mean."

"No, what do you mean?"

"Let's just say, we've closed in on third base, but a grand slam can't be too far in the future."

"That isn't right," Detrich said, a little horrified. "He's using his position over you."

"No, it isn't like that at all," Mark protested. "It's something I want. And something he wants, too. And that way I don't have to do all the crappy stuff the rest of you guys are doing. I don't see anything wrong with giving a little pleasure and saving myself a little pain."

"That's what I mean," Detrich said. "He shouldn't be letting you exchange sex for work."

"You're just jealous your guy isn't gay and gorgeous," Mark said, obviously getting angry.

"No, I mean, he's using his power over you to get…"

"It isn't sex," Mark interrupted. "It's just a blow job, and it's something we both enjoy, as men, of our own free will. Fire just might be my happily ever after, and I'm not going to let you get in the way of things. It's really none of your business! I shouldn't have told you anything!"

"You're right," Detrich said, holding his hands in the air in surrender. "It's not my business. But if there's a real relationship happening between you guys, he should wait until you're a full member of the fraternity before moving forward. That's all I'm saying. He shouldn't be taking advantage of his position. But if you're cool with it, I won't say another word."

"Good. So we can let this go?" Mark asked, still clearly upset.

"Yeah, man, you do you."

From then on, Detrich tried not to notice the many subtle moves of affection Mark gave to Fire, or the way Fire seemed to use that attraction to convince Mark to do random humiliating things in front of the other guys. He'd be asked to serve as a footstool during long meetings, required to moan in appreciation when he was paddled any time any of the other pledges did something wrong, and told to act like a "good little kitten" by crawling on hands and knees and rubbing up against Fire's leg while the other guys were busy doing the landscaping.

He tried to ignore it because Mark continued to confide

in Detrich about how happy he was with the way his relationship with Fire was developing. Unlike Detrich, Mark had roommates, but they weren't gay. Detrich guessed that was why Mark opened up to him more about his relationship with Fire. Or maybe it was because Detrich had caught him in that unguarded moment and knew about the relationship they were trying to keep secret.

Nothing about the situation looked healthy to Detrich, but he didn't know Mark all that well, so it didn't feel right to step in, either. Keeping his promise, after that first conversation, Detrich didn't mention his own feelings on the topic again.

It was just past midterms when there was a sudden shift in Mark's attitude. Fire also seemed to be getting a little extra-harsh on his "Kitten," no longer letting him play petting games. Instead, he kept finding hard, dirty manual work for Mark to do.

Detrich was afraid to ask what was going on, but after another late night of Uber driving, he dropped Wind off at the house to find Mark sitting on the front steps, too tired to walk back to his shared apartment.

"You might have been right," Mark suddenly spat into the quiet of the car during the ride back to Mark's place.

"What do you mean?" Detrich asked, his mind already spinning forward to the assignment he still had to finish that night.

"I thought we had something building, but you might

have been right about Fire. I think he might have been just using me."

"What happened?"

"It started a week or so ago. Just before midterms. Fire was stressed about his exams and wanted my help to blow off a little steam." Mark paused and looked over at Detrich.

Detrich gave a little nod to let his friend know he was capable of reading between the lines.

"The only thing was, we were in the main lounge, and there was another frat brother in there with us." Mark paused as Detrich pulled into a parking spot in front of Mark's apartment.

Detrich put the car in park and shifted in his seat, letting his friend know he was willing to stay and listen.

"I thought we would be going to his room, but Fire said no. He needed to stay with his books. He wanted me to get under the table, like a kitten, and lick him from there. It felt odd, having his friend there and all, but at the same time, it was kinda hot, you know? To have someone else there and watching?"

Mark looked at Detrich again, as if for confirmation. Detrich didn't know what to say, so he just sat there and looked back at Mark.

"Fire started getting hot with me just licking him, so he pushed back from the table and undid his pants the rest of the way. 'Here, Kitten,' he called to me, and I crawled out to him with the friend still looking on. Then he had me go full on, even grabbed my hair when he wanted me to go deeper. It wasn't until after he came that he let me come up, but he kept his grip on my hair. Then he turned my head to see his friend, sitting real close with his crotch already near my face and holding himself ready. 'Do my friend,' Fire said, and he pushed my head over."

Mark stopped to take in a shaky breath.

"I didn't even know the guy," he said. "I still don't know his name. I know lots of guys who roll that way, not really caring as long as they get their kicks, but that's not me. I thought we had something. I thought we were building something. But I felt nothing for the other guy. Not even close to my type. That's when I realized, maybe you were right all along. Maybe Fire was just using me. I-I just couldn't do it."

"What happened?" Detrich couldn't stop himself from asking.

"I refused. I clammed up and pushed back. Fire let me go, but he was angry. He said if I wanted my easy ride into the frat, I'd better do what he said, but I just couldn't. Things have been different ever since. I don't know. Maybe I read things wrong. Maybe he needed me to prove my love."

"No, man, that's not how love works," Detrich said. "I don't know if there's a chance for you and Fire, but if there is, it can't be based on that, on you sacrificing yourself like that. He has to respect your boundaries."

"Yeah, I guess you're right. I really thought this might be my big college romance."

"What are you going to do now?"

"There's only a few more weeks before finals," Mark said. "Maybe after a little time, Fire will calm down and we can work this out. I probably just embarrassed him when he couldn't control me like he said. I'm sure that's it. Things will get better again once I'm a full brother."

Detrich couldn't believe what he was hearing. This was clearly a violation of some kind.

"Mark, I don't think . . ."

"No, I don't want to hear it," Mark interrupted him. "Thanks for listening, but I think I've got it worked out for myself. Fire was embarrassed and now he's mad, but he'll get over it. In the meantime, I need to pay my dues like all the other pledges have been doing all along and, once I'm a full brother, we can pick up where we left off. Thanks for the ride, I'm beat."

With that, Mark got out of the car and shut the door behind him. Detrich saw no option but to head back to his dorm and his homework.

Things did not seem to let up for Mark in the next couple of weeks, but he never complained. He didn't confide in Detrich about any further incidents with Fire.

Detrich thought about going to Mr. Cortez with the information he had, but it really wasn't his place. It should be Mark going to the advisor. If Detrich said anything, it was just as likely that both Fire and Mark would deny it, and then Detrich would be the one left in the dorms. Since nothing else seemed to be happening, Detrich decided to focus on trying to keep up his GPA through the final weeks of the semester.

Hell week arrived without further incident. Detrich had a week left to get his final projects completed before finals and was struggling to focus with Carl's non-stop gaming. It seemed his roommate had decided to blow off this semester in favor of a Final Fantasy marathon.

Detrich was only about a third of the way through his biggest project when Wind came storming through his door once again with the pillowcase. As they drove around in the van, the big brothers entertained the pledges with horror stories of pledge night. The guys endured hours of questions, running, beatings, and more running.

Finally, the last question was answered to the brothers' satisfaction, and the blindfolds came off. Detrich opened his eyes to see they were in a warehouse of some kind and folding tables had been set up with the kegs already flowing.

"You made it, bitches," Fire called out, holding a red party cup in the air in salute. "All that's left now is the formalities. Welcome to Beta Epsilon Omega, brothers!"

With a broad smile, Detrich joined in the celebration, accepting a party cup from Wind and downing it in a gulp. The rest of the night was a blur. Detrich wasn't even sure how he got back to his dorm room, but that's where he woke up the next morning with one of the worst hangovers he'd ever had. It took until afternoon before he could see straight again, but by then, he'd already heard from all his new frat brothers about how sick the party had been the night before. They were all glad the official crossing over ceremony wouldn't be held until Sunday night, so they'd have the full weekend to recover.

It wasn't until Sunday morning that Detrich realized he still hadn't heard from Mark. Flashes of Mark cozying up to Fire toward the end of the party crossed his mind, but Detrich hoped Mark hadn't been foolish enough to try rekindling their relationship already. He decided to give his friend a call.

"Lo?" Mark's voice answered the line, sounding deeper and slower than usual.

"Mark, is that you?"

"My phone, my choice," Mark's voice responded, but it sounded so wrong.

"Hey, man, just checking in with you. Are you excited about the ceremony tonight?"

"Ceremony? Sacrifice! Soul is lost, it's not worth it." Mark wasn't making any sense, but before Detrich could try to get anything else out of him, the line went dead.

Detrich tried to call a few more times, but Mark wasn't picking up anymore. Since he didn't know any of the roommates' phone numbers, Detrich decided to head over to talk to Mark in person. Something was definitely wrong.

On arriving, one of Mark's roommates let him in without any complaint but mentioned he didn't even think Mark was home. None of them had seen him since he left Friday night. Detrich made his way back to Mark's room to find it in an absolute mess, which was completely out of character for his fastidious friend. Detrich's eyes widened when he recognized the midnight blue and white colors of a fraternity sweat suit scattered across the floor. None of the pledges were supposed to have access to fraternity colors until after the official ceremony that evening, but these clothes had been shredded into rags that were scattered to every corner of the room.

"Mark, are you here?" Detrich called out.

"Here!" Mark's voice called out from the attached bathroom.

"What's with the sweat suit?"

"A present from Fire."

"Why would he give you a present before we're allowed to have it?" Detrich asked through the door.

"He was happy with me," Mark's voice still sounded slurred and cracked at the last statement. The sound of it sent a shiver of dread through Detrich.

"What happened?"

"That other guy," Mark mumbled. "He's Fire's boyfriend. They're together. They've always been together."

"You caught them together at the party?" Detrich asked. He was still trying to figure out why the track suit was torn to shreds.

"You were right," Mark's voice was quieter. It was growing

more slurred as he talked, making it hard for Detrich to understand him through the bathroom door. "He knew I liked him. He liked controlling me. I was such a fool. I didn't even think. I didn't even taste it. But it had to be him."

"What do you mean?" Detrich demanded. "I can't even hear you through this door." In anger, Detrich pushed the bathroom door open and saw, to his horror, Mark sitting naked in the tub, the water already red with blood from the gashes on his wrists.

"Such a fool," Mark said, looking up at Detrich. "Can't do this."

"Call 911," Detrich yelled to Mark's roommates in the other room. One of them came running in to see what was happening and immediately grabbed Mark's phone lying on the bathroom floor next to the tub to make the call.

Mark's eyes were falling closed and Detrich grabbed a towel to press to the gash in his arm, trying to stop the bleeding.

"Stay with me, Mark. Tell me what happened," Detrich demanded, slapping his friend lightly across the face to get his attention.

In fits and spurts, Detrich finally pieced together the story. Sometime during the party, Mark tried to rekindle his friendship with Fire, which Fire encouraged enough to get Mark to go back to the frat house.

While Mark clearly thought they were starting the relationship he'd been hoping for all along, it was a surprise to him to see Fire's other friend at the frat house, too, along with some of the other guys. There'd been some kind of toast with drinks Fire had mixed up at the frat's wet bar. There might have been more drinks after that, but Mark couldn't remember. His story went fuzzy at that point.

It seemed clear Fire had mixed something into Mark's drink to make him pass out. Mark remembered moments of passion through the night, but none of the details. When he woke up Saturday morning, he was bruised, sore, and naked in bed with Fire's friend, the man he'd rejected before.

"I wouldn't have done that," Mark kept muttering. "That's not me. I wouldn't have done it. I was so stupid. I'm too stupid to live."

Just as he was making sense of the story, the paramedics arrived and took over Mark's triage. Detrich was glad to step back and let them work. They quickly hauled Mark out of the tub and onto the stretcher to rush him to the emergency room. They couldn't tell Detrich what Mark's true condition might be, but their serious expressions and urgency spoke louder than words. If Mark survived, it would be a close call.

Sitting among the tatters of the fraternity sweat suit in Mark's room, Detrich wondered if it had just been the one guy who had taken advantage of Mark or if there were more involved. He wondered what kind of fraternity he was getting involved with that would allow a guy like Fire to be in it. Could he trust joining a group that had allowed such a thing to happen? Or was it just one bad apple in the bunch? Should he go to the advisor with what he knew? Would that change anything?

Story Terrace

www.ingramcontent.com/pod-product-compliance
Lightning Source LLC
LaVergne TN
LVHW061631070526
838199LV00071B/6646